GUIDE TO CAPTAIN AMERICA:

BRAVE NEW WORLD

Everything You Need to Know About

the MCU's Film

Taylor Cross

© Copyright taylorcross 2024

All rights reserved. No part of this publication may be reproduced, distributed, or transmitted in any form or by any means, including photocopying, recording, or other electronic or mechanical methods, without the prior written permission of the publisher, except in the case of brief quotations embodied in critical reviews and certain other noncommercial uses permitted by copyright law.

Disclaimer:

This is an unofficial movie guide for Captain America: Brave New World. It is not authorized, endorsed, or affiliated with Marvel Studios, Walt Disney Studios Motion Pictures, or any associated entities. All movie content, characters, and trademarks are the property of their respective owners. This guide serves as a fan-created resource to enrich your experience with the film.

ISBN: 9798306716831
Imprint: Independently published

Table of Contents

Guide to Captain America: Brave New World 1

    Everything You Need to Know About the MCU's Most Anticipated Film 1

Introduction 4

Premise 10

Cast of Captain America: Brave New World 18

Production and Development 30

    Pre-Production 34

    Filming Process 37

    Post-Production Challenges and Reshoots 40

    Visual Effects and Editing 43

Music 45

Marketing 46

Release 51

Conclusion 53

Introduction

The Marvel Cinematic Universe (MCU) has been a dominant force in shaping modern cinematic storytelling, captivating audiences worldwide with its intricate narratives and dynamic characters. Among its most celebrated heroes is Captain America, a symbol of resilience, leadership, and hope. With the upcoming release of Captain America: Brave New World on February 14, 2025, Marvel Studios is set to usher in a thrilling new chapter in this iconic saga. This film not only continues the legacy of the Captain America film series but also marks a pivotal moment in the

MCU, blending elements of political intrigue, global stakes, and personal growth for its central character, Sam Wilson.

Transitioning from his role as the Falcon to wielding the shield of Captain America, Sam Wilson, portrayed by Anthony Mackie, faces challenges that extend far beyond the battlefield. Following the events of The Falcon and the Winter Soldier (2021), Wilson steps fully into his role as the new Captain America, tasked with navigating a world rife with political tension and moral ambiguity. Directed by Julius Onah, with a screenplay co-written by Peter Glanz and Matthew Orton, Captain America: Brave New World promises a gripping narrative that explores the complexities of heroism in an ever-changing global landscape.

This fourth installment in the Captain America film series introduces a stellar ensemble cast, including returning MCU veterans and fresh faces. Notably, the film features Harrison Ford as Thaddeus Ross, stepping into the role previously held by the late William Hurt. Ford's portrayal of Ross as the President of the United

States—and his transformation into the formidable Red Hulk—adds layers of political and emotional depth to the story. Alongside Mackie, the cast includes Danny Ramirez, Carl Lumbly, Shira Haas, Giancarlo Esposito, and Tim Blake Nelson, whose characters promise to enrich the narrative with intrigue and conflict.

Filming for Brave New World took place across notable locations such as Atlanta, Georgia, and Washington, D.C., enhancing the film's authentic and grounded feel. From its initial conceptualization in 2021 to the reshoots in 2024, the film underwent meticulous development, ensuring a polished and compelling addition to the MCU. The shift in the film's subtitle from New World Order to Brave New World during production signifies its emphasis on exploring new horizons and redefining what it means to be Captain America in the modern era.

As a continuation of the MCU's Phase Five, Captain America: Brave New World holds the promise of delivering an experience that is both action-packed and thought-provoking. With its strong ties to the events of previous films and series, the movie sets the stage for a narrative that seamlessly intertwines personal struggles with global challenges. This guide serves as an essential companion for fans and newcomers alike, diving into the film's development, cast, themes, and its anticipated impact on the MCU's ever-expanding universe. Prepare to witness a Captain America story like no other—a brave new world awaits.

PREMISE

Captain America: Brave New World presents a gripping storyline that places Sam Wilson, the newly appointed Captain America, in the midst of an international crisis. The film takes place following the election of Thaddeus Ross as the president of the United States, a pivotal political shift that has far-reaching consequences for both the MCU and the world at large. As the story unfolds, Sam Wilson, portrayed by Anthony Mackie, finds himself caught at the center of a high-stakes global conflict, where he must navigate complex political landscapes while uncovering a deeper conspiracy that threatens not only the United States but also international peace.

Thaddeus Ross, once a military general and a key figure in the MCU, has ascended to the presidency. His election marks a significant shift in the political dynamics of the MCU, and with it comes the weight of responsibility that comes with leading a nation in a turbulent world. However, Ross's rise to power also brings with it the emergence of new threats, both from within the United States and from global actors with far-reaching ambitions. As president, Ross must deal with the challenges of maintaining global stability while grappling with his own transformation into the Red Hulk, a powerful and unpredictable force that complicates his presidency and his role as a leader.

Sam Wilson, now fully embracing his role as Captain America, finds himself in the middle of this international incident. His journey is deeply personal, as he struggles with the weight of the mantle of Captain America and the moral dilemmas that come with it. Sam is not just fighting for justice on the battlefield; he is working to protect the ideals of freedom and democracy that Captain America has always stood for. When an international crisis erupts, Sam is thrust into a political game that tests his ability to navigate the complex and often murky world of global diplomacy, espionage, and covert operations.

The core of the story revolves around Sam Wilson's quest to uncover the true masterminds behind the international incident. As the situation escalates, Sam discovers that the crisis is not simply a series of isolated events but part of a larger, more sinister plan orchestrated by forces operating behind the scenes. These masterminds, whose motives remain shrouded in secrecy, are using the global unrest to further their own agendas, and it is up to Sam to stop them before they can achieve their goals and plunge the world into chaos.

Sam's struggle is not just one of physical combat but also one of intelligence and strategy. He must rely on his instincts, his training, and his unwavering moral compass to uncover the truth. Alongside his allies, including old friends from The Falcon and the Winter Soldier and new faces who join him on his mission, Sam faces numerous obstacles. These challenges include confronting powerful enemies, navigating the shifting allegiances of world leaders, and dealing with the personal toll that comes with being a symbol of hope and justice in such uncertain times.

As the film progresses, the stakes grow higher, and Sam's resolve is tested like never before. The situation is not just about saving the day in traditional superhero fashion; it's about understanding the complexities of global politics, the consequences of unchecked power, and the sacrifices required to protect the greater good. Sam's journey is one of self-discovery, as he learns what it truly means to be Captain America—not just a hero in a suit, but a leader who must make tough choices in the face of overwhelming odds.

In the end, Captain America: Brave New World is more than just a superhero film. It is a story about leadership, responsibility, and the courage to fight for what is right, no matter the cost. Sam

Wilson's journey to stop the true masterminds behind the international incident will not only test his strength but also his character, and the film promises to deliver a thrilling, emotionally charged narrative that will leave audiences eagerly anticipating the next chapter in the MCU.

Cast of Captain America: Brave New World

Captain America: Brave New World boasts a stellar cast led by Anthony Mackie, who reprises his role as Sam Wilson / Captain America. Known for his portrayal of the former Falcon, Mackie's character has now fully embraced the mantle of Captain America. Producer Nate Moore describes Wilson's journey as that of an underdog, much like the iconic Rocky Balboa. Unlike Steve Rogers, Wilson doesn't have super-soldier serum-enhanced abilities or a vast network of allies; instead, he must rely on his sharp instincts, personal strength, and the vibranium shield and wing suit to level the playing field. According to Mackie, Wilson's interpretation of Captain America will be different—he will not be judgmental, possessing a unique understanding of good and bad, far removed from the traditional hero archetype. This evolution of Sam Wilson into a strong leader reflects his journey to becoming a hero on his own terms.

Danny Ramirez as Joaquin Torres / Falcon

Danny Ramirez plays Joaquin Torres, a first lieutenant in the U.S. Air Force, who assumes the mantle of Falcon after Wilson's transformation into Captain America. Torres is portrayed as a close companion to Wilson, with their friendship characterized by mutual respect and equality. This marks a departure from the previous dynamic between Wilson and Steve Rogers in the MCU. Mackie even gave Ramirez tips on wearing the Falcon suit, highlighting the camaraderie between the two characters both on and off-screen.

Shira Haas as Ruth Bat-Seraph

Shira Haas portrays Ruth Bat-Seraph, an Israeli former Black Widow who has risen to become a high-ranking U.S. government official. Ruth is a trusted ally of President Thaddeus Ross, and her character brings a unique blend of international experience and covert operations to the story. Haas's portrayal promises a complex and nuanced character, adding depth to the film's political intrigue.

Carl Lumbly as Isaiah Bradley

Carl Lumbly returns as Isaiah Bradley, an African-American Korean War veteran and super soldier who endured experimentation and imprisonment for 30 years. His character adds a layer of historical depth to the narrative, touching on themes of injustice and sacrifice. Isaiah Bradley's presence in the story is important, especially in the context of Sam Wilson's journey as Captain America, as Bradley represents both the legacy of past heroes and the scars left by a fractured history.

Xosha Roquemore as a Secret Service Agent

Xosha Roquemore plays a Secret Service agent, whose role in the plot remains mysterious.

Roquemore's character is likely to be involved in the high-stakes political drama surrounding President Ross, adding an air of suspense and danger to the unfolding events.

Jóhannes Haukur Jóhannesson

While the specifics of Jóhannes Haukur Jóhannesson's role are unclear, his inclusion in the cast suggests he will be part of the expanding roster of characters involved in the international conflict Sam Wilson faces.

Giancarlo Esposito as Seth Voelker / Sidewinder

Giancarlo Esposito takes on the role of Seth Voelker, also known as Sidewinder, the leader of the Serpent Society. Esposito's portrayal promises to bring his trademark intensity to the role of a highly intelligent and physically imposing antagonist. Describing Voelker as an intelligent "badass," Esposito reveals that his character will be a formidable foe for Sam Wilson. The physicality of the role sets Voelker apart from Esposito's previous roles, particularly Gus Fring in Breaking Bad.

Tim Blake Nelson as Samuel Sterns / Leader

Tim Blake Nelson reprises his role as Samuel Sterns, a cellular biologist whose exposure to Bruce Banner's blood gave him superhuman intelligence. As the Leader, Nelson's character will serve as a brilliant yet dangerous adversary for Wilson. The film will delve into Sterns's pathos and rage, shedding light on his evolution since his last appearance in The Incredible Hulk (2008). Nelson's portrayal of Sterns, with his more comic-accurate look, promises a compelling antagonist driven by intellect.

Harrison Ford as Thaddeus "Thunderbolt" Ross / Red Hulk

Harrison Ford steps into the role of Thaddeus Ross, who has now ascended to the presidency of the United States. Ross's transformation into Red Hulk adds another layer of complexity to his character. Ford's portrayal of the character highlights a dynamic shift, as Ross, once an antagonist hunting down the Hulk, now finds himself in a position of power. His relationship with Sam Wilson is expected to be filled with tension, especially given the events of Captain America: Civil War (2016). Ford's Red Hulk will be brought to life using motion capture technology, enhancing the character's physical presence.

Liv Tyler as Betty Ross

Liv Tyler returns as Betty Ross, a cellular biologist and Thaddeus Ross's daughter. Tyler's character will add an emotional and personal dimension to the story, especially as she navigates the complex dynamics between her father and the heroes of the MCU.

Rosa Salazar as Diamondback

Rosa Salazar plays Diamondback, a member of the Serpent Society. As a formidable foe in her own right, Diamondback's inclusion in the film suggests that the Serpent Society will play a significant role in the conflict, adding another layer of intrigue to the story.

Takehiro Hira as Prime Minister Ozaki

Takehiro Hira plays Prime Minister Ozaki, a political figure whose role in the story is pivotal to the international stakes at play. His involvement with the global crisis, particularly in relation to President Ross, promises to escalate the tension and intrigue surrounding Sam Wilson's mission.

With such a talented ensemble cast, Captain America: Brave New World is set to be an exciting and emotionally charged film, blending action, political drama, and superhero thrills. The film's rich character dynamics, coupled with the complex web of alliances and rivalries, will no doubt captivate audiences as Sam Wilson steps into his new role as Captain America.

Production and Development

In **October 2015**, Kevin Feige, the president of Marvel Studios, said that **Captain America: Civil War** (2016) was the final movie in the Captain America trilogy, which also included **Captain America: The First Avenger** (2011) and **Captain America: The Winter Soldier** (2014). These films starred **Chris Evans** as Steve Rogers / Captain America. Although **Civil War** was Evans's last solo Captain America movie under contract, he was open to staying longer in the Marvel Cinematic Universe (MCU) for movies like

Avengers: Infinity War (2018) and Avengers: Endgame (2019). In January 2021, there were reports that Evans might return as Steve Rogers for at least one future Marvel project, playing a smaller role like Robert Downey Jr. did as Iron Man in other MCU films. However, Evans denied these reports, saying they were "news to [him]."

In October 2018, Marvel Studios started working on a Disney+ series starring Anthony Mackie as Sam Wilson / Falcon and Sebastian Stan as Bucky Barnes / Winter Soldier. Malcolm Spellman was hired as the main writer, and the show was officially announced in April 2019 as

The Falcon and the Winter Soldier. After Steve Rogers passed his shield and the Captain America title to Sam Wilson in **Endgame**, the series focused on Sam coming to terms with taking on this role, especially as a Black man.

Before the series was released, Mackie said there were no plans yet for a second season, and he didn't know when he would appear next in an MCU movie due to the COVID-19 pandemic. The show's director, **Kari Skogland**, and executive producer, **Nate Moore**, said there were still many stories to explore, but they weren't sure about a second season. Marvel Studios wanted the show to lead into a movie, like they did with **WandaVision** (2021).

After the final episode of **The Falcon and the Winter Soldier** aired in **April 2021**, Spellman and writer **Dalan Musson** started working on a fourth Captain America movie, continuing Sam Wilson's story. Mackie was excited about the possibility of leading an MCU film as a Black actor. He signed on to star in the movie in **August 2021**, though he admitted he was initially disappointed because he was hoping for a second season of the Disney+ series with Stan and their co-star **Daniel Brühl** (who played the villain Zemo).

Pre-Production

Mackie confirmed that the movie would be a new story with new characters, not just a continuation of **The Falcon and the Winter Soldier**. In **July 2022, Julius Onah** was hired as the director, and the movie's title, **Captain America: New World Order**, was revealed at San Diego Comic-Con. It was set to release on **May 3, 2024**, as part of the MCU's Phase Five. The title sparked controversy due to its connections to politics, conspiracy theories, and antisemitic rhetoric.

At the **D23 Expo** in **September 2022**, several cast members were announced:

- **Danny Ramirez** as Joaquin Torres / Falcon

- **Carl Lumbly** as Isaiah Bradley

- **Tim Blake Nelson** returning as Samuel Sterns / Leader from **The Incredible Hulk** (2008)

- **Shira Haas** as Ruth Bat-Seraph, a new version of the Israeli superhero Sabra.

The inclusion of Sabra, an Israeli character, drew criticism from some groups, who felt her portrayal could lead to negative stereotypes of Palestinians and Arabs. Marvel responded by saying they were reimagining the character for modern audiences, which upset some supporters of Israel who wanted her to retain her original comic book backstory. Despite the backlash, both the **American Jewish Committee (AJC)** and the **Anti-Defamation League (ADL)** praised Marvel for keeping the character Israeli.

In **October 2022, Harrison Ford** was cast as **Thaddeus "Thunderbolt" Ross**, replacing **William Hurt**, who played the character before his death in March 2022. Ford would also appear as Ross in the upcoming MCU film **Thunderbolts** (2025). In the new movie, Ross becomes the President of the United States and clashes with Sam Wilson amidst a global conspiracy. The story was compared to the **Secret Empire** comic book storyline.

Filming Process

The filming of *Captain America: Brave New World* began on March 21, 2023, at Trilith Studios in Atlanta, Georgia. The project initially operated under the working title *Rochelle Rochelle*. The cinematographer for the film was Kramer Morgenthau, whose work aimed to deliver a grounded and tactile action aesthetic. Director Julius Onah wanted the film to stand apart from previous Marvel Cinematic Universe (MCU) films by incorporating more practical effects and action sequences. The goal was to present Sam Wilson, the new Captain America, in a way that showcased fresh, action-packed scenarios that audiences had not seen in his earlier appearances.

Liv Tyler joined the cast in late March 2023, reprising her role as Betty Ross from *The Incredible Hulk* (2008). Around this time, Julia Louis-Dreyfus was also expected to return as Valentina Allegra de Fontaine. Despite the Writers Guild of America strike starting in May 2023, filming continued as planned, with Marvel Studios ensuring they captured what they could during principal photography and prepared for any necessary rewrites or reshoots later. In May, set photos revealed Seth Rollins as part of the cast, leading to speculation about his role as a member of the Serpent Society.

In June 2023, Marvel Studios announced a title change for the movie, renaming it *Captain America: Brave New World*. This new title was praised for its optimistic tone, replacing the original title, *New World Order*, which some critics felt could carry negative connotations. Marvel Studios explained that the change reflected feedback and ensured the title did not inadvertently evoke real-world controversies. Filming subsequently moved to Washington, D.C., and wrapped on June 30, 2023.

Post-Production Challenges and Reshoots

Post-production for *Brave New World* faced a few hurdles, including delays caused by the SAG-AFTRA strike in 2023. Initially slated for a May 2024 release, the film was later postponed to February 14, 2025, due to production setbacks. Early test screenings reportedly received mixed reactions, prompting Marvel Studios to plan extensive reshoots from early 2024 to mid-2024. These reshoots aimed to refine certain sequences and incorporate additional material to enhance the storyline.

In December 2023, Matthew Orton, known for his work on the Marvel series *Moon Knight*, was hired to write new material for the reshoots. Rosa Salazar was also confirmed to play a significant role, later revealed as Diamondback, a member of the Serpent Society. Giancarlo Esposito joined the cast as Seth Voelker, also known as Sidewinder, the leader of the Serpent Society.

Reshoots began in May 2024 in Atlanta and were completed after 22 days. These additional scenes were designed to improve the action sequences and integrate Esposito's character more effectively. Anthony Mackie clarified that the reshoots were not intended to overhaul the movie but rather to enhance specific aspects. The storyline also introduced the remains of Tiamut, a Celestial from *Eternals* (2021), as a plot device to bring the fictional metal adamantium into the MCU.

Visual Effects and Editing

The visual effects team, led by Alessandro Ongaro, collaborated with several renowned studios, including Wētā FX, Digital Domain, and Luma Pictures. Wētā FX played a key role in designing the Red Hulk, ensuring the character's appearance was both intimidating and distinct from the Hulk. Harrison Ford's facial features were incorporated into the design, adding a personal touch to Red Hulk's military-inspired aesthetic. The climactic battle between Red Hulk and Captain America in Washington, D.C., was a visually demanding sequence involving over 300 visual effects shots.

The film's editing was handled by Matthew Schmidt and Madeleine Gavin. Schmidt, who had previously worked on *Captain America: The Winter Soldier* and *Civil War*, brought his expertise to the project. The combination of advanced visual effects and precise editing aimed to deliver a high-quality cinematic experience.

Music

The music for *Captain America: Brave New World* is composed by Laura Karpman, a name familiar to fans of the Marvel Cinematic Universe (MCU). Karpman has a history of creating powerful and engaging scores, including her work on the animated series *What If...?* (2021-2024), the Disney+ show *Ms. Marvel* (2022), and the film *The Marvels* (2023). Her return to Marvel for this project promises another memorable musical experience that will enhance the film's tone and storytelling.

Marketing

Marketing for the film began with a bang at CinemaCon in April 2024, where Marvel Studios head Kevin Feige and lead actor Anthony Mackie revealed the first footage. This footage gave fans a glimpse of Sam Wilson's Captain America meeting with President Thaddeus Ross, generating excitement and speculation about the storyline.

In May 2024, McDonald's joined the marketing campaign by introducing Happy Meals featuring toys of characters from the film. Notably, these toys included characters like Red Hulk and

Diamondback, whose appearances in the movie had not yet been confirmed at the time. The early release of these toys was likely due to the film's delayed release while the McDonald's promotional schedule remained unchanged.

Additional footage was shown at CineEurope in June, further building anticipation. In July, the first teaser trailer was released, drawing comparisons to the critically acclaimed *Captain America: The Winter Soldier*. Critics noted its mix of superhero action and political thriller elements. The trailer sparked widespread discussion about Red Hulk's role in the film, with fans speculating about the character's identity. Some wondered if President Ross would transform into Red Hulk, while others suspected a surprise twist.

The trailer also revealed significant story elements, including the remains of the Celestial Tiamut from *Eternals*. This revelation highlighted a Global Unity Summit, where nations like the United States and Japan discuss the Celestial's body. The summit's logo, a stylized version of Tiamut's hand, added a unique visual element to the trailer.

Marvel promoted the film at San Diego Comic-Con in July 2024, where more footage was shown, and Giancarlo Esposito's role was announced. It was also confirmed that Thaddeus Ross would indeed transform into Red Hulk. Following leaks of the Comic-Con and D23 Expo footage, Marvel officially revealed Red Hulk in an anniversary video celebrating the company's 85 years.

In November, a full trailer premiered at D23 Brasil and was later released online. This trailer showcased Red Hulk's transformation and his intense battle with Sam Wilson. Critics praised the trailer for its unique style, including split-screen shots and flickering text effects. The film was compared to classic political thrillers like *The Parallax View* (1974) and *All the President's Men* (1976), setting high expectations for its tone and narrative depth.

Release

Captain America: Brave New World is set to hit theaters on February 14, 2025, with an IMAX release. The film's release has seen several delays, originally planned for May 3, 2024, and then July 26, 2024. The delays were due to the 2023 SAG-AFTRA strike. As part of Phase Five of the MCU, this movie is expected to play a significant role in continuing the overarching Marvel storyline.

Final Thoughts

With its intriguing storyline, exciting marketing campaign, and strong musical foundation, *Captain

America: Brave New World is shaping up to be a must-watch film for MCU fans. Whether it's the political thriller elements, the return of beloved characters, or the introduction of Red Hulk, the film promises a fresh and thrilling addition to the Marvel Cinematic Universe.

Conclusion

Captain America: Brave New World is poised to be a pivotal chapter in the Marvel Cinematic Universe, blending action, political intrigue, and deep character development. With Laura Karpman's powerful score setting the tone, a marketing campaign that has already sparked excitement, and an intriguing narrative that ties together unresolved threads from past Marvel films, the movie has all the ingredients to captivate both longtime fans and newcomers.

The film's exploration of global tensions, the emergence of new threats like Red Hulk, and the continuation of Sam Wilson's journey as Captain America reflect Marvel's commitment to storytelling that resonates on both personal and global levels. Its mix of superhero spectacle and a grounded, political thriller vibe suggests an evolution for the franchise, drawing comparisons to some of cinema's most iconic political dramas.

As part of Phase Five of the MCU, *Captain America: Brave New World* is not just another superhero film—it's a story of leadership, unity, and the challenges of living up to a legacy. With its February 2025 release, fans can look forward to a film that honors Marvel's past while paving

the way for its future.

Made in the USA
Columbia, SC
16 February 2025